AI Influencer Marketing

Find, Collaborate, and Scale Partnerships Using Data

By Joe Correa

Published by Live Stronger Faster

This book is for educational and informational purposes only. The author and publisher are not engaged in rendering legal, financial, or other professional advice. Readers should consult a qualified professional before making any financial decisions.

First Edition

Table of Contents

Introduction

Influencer marketing has always been about connection — finding voices that resonate with audiences and brands that align with those voices. But what once relied heavily on intuition, guesswork, and endless scrolling through social feeds has now evolved into a precise, data-driven science powered by artificial intelligence. Today, AI influencer marketing has become one of the most effective and scalable ways to build trust, drive sales, and create authentic engagement at a global level. It's not just about hiring influencers anymore; it's about building intelligent partnerships based on measurable impact, predictive analytics, and automated collaboration systems that save time, reduce risk, and multiply ROI.

In the past, brands would manually search for influencers, negotiate rates, and hope their campaigns performed. The process was inefficient, filled with fake followers, and hard to measure. But AI has completely rewritten that story. Using AI influencer finder tools and social data analysis, businesses can now identify the right influencers for their exact audience, automatically vet engagement quality, and even predict future performance. Instead of chasing vanity metrics like follower counts, AI allows marketers to analyze true influence — how much trust an influencer's content generates, what kind of actions their audience takes, and how much revenue their posts are likely to produce. With AI sponsorship tools, the entire influencer marketing lifecycle — from discovery to ROI tracking — can now be automated.

At the core of AI influencer marketing lies one key principle: alignment between brand message and audience psychology. Artificial intelligence analyzes billions of interactions across platforms like Instagram, YouTube, TikTok, and X (formerly Twitter) to understand how content travels, how emotions influence buying behavior, and which creators are most likely to generate engagement from a specific demographic. This is a level of precision that no human team could ever replicate manually. For example, a skincare company looking for micro-influencers among 25- to 40-year-old women who value cruelty-free products can instantly receive a curated list of creators whose audience fits that profile — complete with sentiment analysis, engagement health, and projected campaign ROI.

The future of influencer marketing is predictive and automated. Tools powered by AI don't just look backward at past campaigns; they forecast outcomes before a single dollar is spent. These systems evaluate influencer performance based on audience overlap, historical conversion rates, and engagement consistency. By combining machine learning with social listening, they provide actionable recommendations — suggesting when to post, which influencers to collaborate with, what type of content performs best, and how much to spend for optimal return. Instead of running trial-and-error campaigns, marketers can make confident, data-backed decisions and scale partnerships strategically.

But perhaps the most exciting aspect of AI influencer marketing is its ability to democratize brand collaboration. In the old system, only large brands with big budgets could access top-tier influencers through agencies. Now, AI-driven platforms make it possible for small businesses, solopreneurs, and startups to find niche creators who deliver massive results for minimal cost. AI influencer matchmaking tools eliminate middlemen by connecting brands and creators directly, using algorithms to ensure mutual fit and genuine partnership potential. This not only saves money but also creates more authentic, long-term collaborations where both parties benefit.

Automation has also transformed the campaign management side of influencer marketing. Once an influencer is selected, AI tools can automatically generate contracts, send creative briefs, track deliverables, and collect performance data in real time. Advanced systems use natural language processing to review influencer posts and captions, ensuring that brand messaging remains compliant and consistent across all platforms. AI-powered dashboards then compile campaign analytics, comparing metrics like engagement rate, cost per click, conversion value, and audience sentiment across multiple influencers. The result is a holistic, automated view of campaign performance — something that once required entire teams and weeks of manual reporting.

Beyond efficiency, AI influencer marketing enhances creativity. It empowers brands and creators with data-driven insights to produce content that resonates emotionally while achieving measurable outcomes. AI can generate content ideas, suggest trending topics, optimize captions, and even assist in video editing — freeing influencers to focus on authenticity and storytelling. Meanwhile, brands can use AI sponsorship tools to A/B test creative approaches, identify which messages are most persuasive, and continuously improve campaign performance. Together, these capabilities merge human creativity with artificial intelligence, producing marketing that feels organic yet operates with machine-level precision.

Ethics and transparency are also evolving alongside this transformation. AI's ability to detect fake engagement and fraudulent activity helps maintain integrity across influencer ecosystems. Algorithms can now identify purchased followers, comment pods, and engagement manipulation — protecting brands from wasted budgets and reputational damage. This means that AI influencer marketing doesn't just make campaigns smarter; it makes them fairer. Real influence becomes the defining metric once again, rewarding authenticity over vanity.

For influencers themselves, AI opens new doors to professionalize their businesses. Creators can analyze their own audience data, identify which brands align best, forecast potential earnings, and use AI negotiation assistants to secure fair deals. They can automate content planning, audience engagement, and reporting — effectively running their influencer business like a high-performing digital agency. The collaboration between creators and AI represents a new era where creativity meets analytics, and both thrive in balance.

In this book, you'll explore how to master every stage of AI-powered influencer marketing — from discovery and outreach to collaboration and scaling. You'll learn how to use the latest AI influencer finder platforms to locate perfect brand partners, build personalized outreach campaigns with natural-language prompts, and automate your negotiations and reporting. You'll see how AI sponsorship tools track ROI with precision, how predictive analytics optimize campaigns, and how automation workflows make scaling partnerships effortless. Whether you're a brand seeking exposure or an influencer aiming to grow your income and credibility, the strategies inside will show you how to leverage AI to achieve measurable success faster than ever.

AI influencer marketing represents a profound shift in how partnerships are built and scaled. It replaces uncertainty with intelligence, replaces manual labor with automation, and replaces random collaborations with precise alignment. As AI continues to evolve, influencer marketing will become even more personalized, predictive, and profitable — driven by systems that understand human behavior better than ever before. The days of blind influencer selection are over; the future belongs to those who can harness AI to build meaningful, data-driven relationships at scale. This book is your roadmap to that future — where creativity and technology combine to redefine influence in the digital age.

Chapter 1: The New Era of Data-Driven Influence

Influencer marketing has undergone one of the most dramatic transformations in the entire digital advertising landscape. What began as a social media experiment—brands paying popular creators to endorse products—has now matured into a data-driven ecosystem powered by artificial intelligence. Chapter 1 sets the foundation for this transformation by explaining why AI has become essential for modern influencer marketing, how it eliminates guesswork, and what systems and tools professionals now use to find, analyze, and manage partnerships more efficiently than ever before.

For most of the last decade, influencer campaigns were driven by human observation and intuition. Marketing managers spent hours scrolling through Instagram feeds, manually reviewing metrics like follower counts and engagement rates, and trying to determine whether an influencer's audience aligned with their target demographic. Although many successful partnerships emerged from this approach, it was slow, subjective, and often inaccurate. Fraudulent followers, inflated engagement, and mismatched brand identities frequently caused disappointing results. AI influencer marketing arose from a simple but powerful need: to bring precision, automation, and accountability into what was previously an inconsistent process.

Artificial intelligence brings objectivity into influencer selection. Through advanced data mining and natural language processing, AI platforms analyze millions of posts, captions, hashtags, and interactions in seconds. Instead of relying on superficial statistics, these tools uncover patterns in audience behavior—identifying what type of content resonates, which emotions drive conversions, and what audience segments are most valuable to a brand. For instance, AI can determine that an influencer with only 30,000 followers but a 12% engagement rate in a specific niche will outperform an influencer with half a million followers but weak authenticity signals. This kind of predictive precision ensures that every collaboration delivers measurable value.

Beyond discovery, AI streamlines the entire influencer lifecycle. Once a suitable influencer is identified, AI systems can automatically evaluate follower authenticity, generate smart contracts, suggest compensation ranges based on historical data, and track campaign performance in real time. Automation eliminates tedious administrative work, freeing marketing teams to focus on creative strategy and relationship building. Predictive analytics further enhance decision-making by forecasting which influencers are likely to maintain engagement consistency and which may experience audience fatigue. The result is a continuous feedback loop where campaigns learn from past performance and optimize themselves for future success.

A crucial component of AI influencer marketing is **influencer-audience alignment**. AI doesn't just match demographics—it interprets psychographics and sentiment. Using machine learning algorithms trained on language, emojis, tone, and behavioral cues, these systems can gauge how audiences *feel* about specific topics, brands, or product categories. If a fitness influencer frequently engages with sustainability-minded followers, AI can recommend eco-friendly health brands as natural partners. This form of emotional intelligence enables brands to collaborate with creators whose followers already believe in their message, dramatically increasing trust and conversion potential.

Campaign measurement has also evolved from vanity metrics to actionable intelligence. AI analytics dashboards track every dimension of performance: reach, engagement quality, click-through rate, conversion rate, and return on ad spend (ROAS). But beyond reporting, these tools provide *insight*. They show how certain tones of messaging, posting times, and visual styles influence outcomes. Brands can compare influencer A's audience response pattern to influencer B's and adjust creative direction immediately. Over time, AI refines the entire strategy—suggesting ideal content formats, budget distribution, and influencer diversification to maximize overall ROI.

The integration of AI in influencer marketing has leveled the playing field for smaller businesses and emerging creators. With accessible AI influencer finder tools, even a startup can identify affordable micro-influencers who deliver genuine engagement. This democratization of data means that success is no longer reserved for large corporations with massive budgets. When combined with automation platforms, small marketing teams can run professional-grade influencer programs, measure results with the same precision as Fortune 500 brands, and continuously scale as data accumulates.

However, the rise of AI influencer marketing also introduces new professional responsibilities. Data accuracy, privacy compliance, and ethical use of automation must remain priorities. Transparency between brands, influencers, and audiences fosters long-term credibility. AI should be viewed as a partner that enhances human decision-making, not replaces it. The best campaigns combine data intelligence with authentic relationships—because even the most advanced algorithms cannot substitute for genuine human connection and creativity.

In summary, the first step toward mastering AI influencer marketing is understanding its purpose: to bring efficiency, predictability, and authenticity to digital partnerships. By leveraging AI's ability to process vast amounts of social data, marketers can identify influencers that align with their brand's values, audiences, and objectives with unprecedented accuracy. As you proceed through this book, you will learn how to apply AI to each stage of the influencer marketing process—finding creators, negotiating collaborations, tracking ROI, and automating workflows. Together, these systems represent a new era of precision marketing where every collaboration is informed by evidence, powered by automation, and scaled intelligently for lasting growth.

Elena's Story

When Elena started her natural skincare company, *Pure Origins*, she had one major challenge: visibility. Her products were effective, ethically sourced, and affordable, but breaking through the noise of social media seemed impossible. Every day, she saw influencers promoting dozens of brands, yet she couldn't figure out how to identify which ones could genuinely represent her business. In the early months, she tried running ads manually and even paid a few creators she admired, but sales barely moved. Some influencers had fake followers;

others didn't match her target audience. Frustrated, she wondered if influencer marketing was just a game of luck.

Everything changed when she discovered an AI influencer platform called *ConnectIQ*. The software claimed to analyze social data from millions of creators across Instagram, TikTok, and YouTube to identify the best matches for any product category. Skeptical but desperate for results, Elena uploaded her brand information—age demographics, location, product keywords, and core values. Within minutes, the system presented her with a list of potential influencers ranked by *authenticity score*, *audience sentiment*, and *projected ROI*. She was stunned. Each influencer profile came with engagement analytics, follower authenticity checks, and even predicted conversion rates based on past campaign data.

One influencer stood out: *Sophie*, a micro-creator with 32,000 followers who specialized in sustainable beauty. Her content was consistent, her engagement rate was over 11%, and her audience showed strong interest in eco-friendly products. The AI tool highlighted that 78% of her followers were women between 25 and 40 years old—the exact demographic Elena wanted. Without hesitation, Elena used the platform's built-in negotiation assistant to generate a proposal and contract template. The system automatically suggested a fair collaboration rate and even offered to track performance once the campaign began.

Within two weeks, Sophie posted her first sponsored video featuring Pure Origins' facial serum. The results exceeded expectations. Sales increased by 45% in the first month, and traffic to Elena's website doubled. The AI analytics dashboard tracked every click, comment, and conversion in real time. It showed which regions produced the most sales, which posts performed best, and even which keywords generated the highest engagement. The system recommended that Elena scale the campaign by collaborating with three other influencers whose audiences overlapped only 20% with Sophie's—ensuring wider reach without redundancy.

By month three, Pure Origins had partnered with seven micro-influencers across different niches, from skincare enthusiasts to eco-travel bloggers. The AI tool managed contracts, payments, and reporting automatically. Elena no longer needed to spend hours sending emails or monitoring performance manually. The predictive model suggested when to renew collaborations, when to pause, and how to reallocate budget for maximum ROI. For the first time, influencer marketing felt scientific.

But the transformation wasn't just in numbers—it was in confidence. Elena could finally make decisions based on evidence rather than hope. When her accountant asked how influencer marketing compared to traditional ads, she pulled up the AI dashboard and showed that her influencer campaigns generated a 380% higher ROI than her previous ad spend. What impressed her most was that every influencer she worked with truly believed in her products, and their followers responded with trust and loyalty.

Months later, at an industry conference, Elena was invited to speak about her success. She shared how AI had reshaped her business, showing graphs of engagement growth and automated workflow screenshots. Many attendees were astonished to learn that she managed her entire influencer network with a single employee and an AI system. As she concluded her talk, she summarized her journey in one sentence that resonated with everyone in the room: "I stopped chasing influencers—and started letting AI find the ones who truly believed in my brand."

That realization marked a turning point not just for *Pure Origins*, but for a growing generation of business owners embracing automation. The combination of human creativity and machine intelligence had turned influencer marketing from a guessing game into a scalable, data-driven process. And as Elena looked at her expanding product line and rising sales charts, she knew that the era of data-driven influence had only just begun.

Chapter 2: AI Influencer Discovery Systems and Smart Matching Algorithms

Finding the right influencer has always been the most critical and time-consuming part of a campaign. A single mismatch between a brand and an influencer can waste thousands of dollars and produce no measurable results. Traditional discovery relied on intuition and limited manual research, but artificial intelligence has revolutionized this process through automated data analysis and smart matching algorithms. AI influencer discovery systems now identify, vet, and rank creators based on audience quality, behavioral patterns, and alignment with specific brand goals—all in a fraction of the time it once took a human team.

Modern discovery systems integrate with major social platforms such as Instagram, TikTok, YouTube, and X through APIs. These systems collect enormous datasets that include follower demographics, content engagement, posting frequency, tone of communication, and audience sentiment. AI models then process this data using machine learning techniques like clustering, natural language processing, and computer vision. The result is a comprehensive understanding of both influencer and audience profiles. For example, if a fitness brand wants to reach women aged 30–45 who value organic lifestyles, AI can instantly locate micro-influencers with audiences matching those exact parameters—down to engagement behavior and emotional tone.

At the heart of these systems are **smart matching algorithms** designed to predict compatibility between brand and creator. The process typically begins by analyzing a brand's digital footprint—its tone, values, visuals, and consumer psychology. The AI then compares that information to influencer data, identifying overlaps and potential synergies. Instead of focusing on raw reach or follower count, these algorithms evaluate "influence relevance," meaning the probability that an influencer's audience will take action based on a particular brand message. The matching process uses multiple layers of analysis: demographic fit, psychographic compatibility, topical alignment, and engagement authenticity.

Machine learning models are also trained to detect and filter fraudulent or low-quality influencers. These systems look for red flags such as sudden follower spikes, repetitive comment patterns, or engagement ratios inconsistent with organic growth. They also examine follower geolocation to ensure that audience distribution matches brand targets. AI-driven fraud detection protects brands from investing in fake reach and ensures that every dollar spent produces genuine visibility.

Another major advancement in AI discovery is **predictive performance scoring**. Each influencer is assigned a predictive score that estimates campaign performance before collaboration begins. This score is calculated using historical data, engagement consistency, sentiment trends, and post frequency. The algorithm forecasts expected click-through rates, conversion potential, and return on investment based on similar past campaigns. Brands can then rank influencers by predicted performance rather than subjective preference, transforming influencer selection into a data-backed decision rather than a gamble.

Visual recognition has also become a key factor in AI influencer discovery. Using computer vision technology, systems can analyze thousands of posts to identify recurring objects, settings, and aesthetic themes. This allows AI to match brands not only by audience but by *style*. For instance, a luxury jewelry brand may prefer influencers who use minimalist compositions and soft lighting, while a streetwear brand might look for urban visuals with energetic tones. This level of image-based alignment ensures that influencer-generated content seamlessly integrates with the brand's creative direction.

The integration of natural language processing (NLP) further enhances the quality of matches. NLP allows AI to analyze captions, comments, and tone to evaluate communication style and emotional resonance. It can detect positivity, authenticity, and even humor in an influencer's interactions. By understanding linguistic subtleties, brands can ensure that the voice of the influencer complements their own messaging. This reduces the risk of off-brand communication and strengthens authenticity in sponsored collaborations.

Automation extends beyond discovery into influencer outreach. AI systems can now auto-generate personalized messages, proposals, and contracts based on prior interactions. They can even predict response probability and suggest optimal times for contact. Instead of manually managing hundreds of potential collaborations, marketers can rely on AI-driven CRMs that prioritize high-probability influencers. This allows human teams to focus on creative collaboration while the system handles repetitive tasks.

AI influencer discovery is also evolving into **cross-platform intelligence**. Instead of analyzing each social network in isolation, modern systems integrate performance data from multiple platforms to build a unified creator profile. This helps brands identify influencers who perform well across ecosystems, enabling multi-channel campaigns that deliver consistent messaging and broader reach. Over time, these cross-platform insights reveal which influencers maintain influence beyond individual trends—those who can generate long-term brand loyalty.

As discovery becomes increasingly automated, the role of the marketer shifts from researcher to strategist. AI takes care of the heavy data work, but human expertise remains essential for interpreting results and nurturing relationships. Smart marketers use AI insights not just to find influencers, but to understand them—what motivates them, what their audiences expect, and how to co-create content that delivers mutual value. When data meets empathy, partnerships evolve beyond transactions and into genuine collaborations.

In short, AI influencer discovery systems and smart matching algorithms are the foundation of scalable influencer marketing. They replace randomness with precision, intuition with intelligence, and inefficiency with automation. By mastering these systems, marketers can eliminate guesswork and consistently identify ideal partners who deliver measurable impact. The next step is to understand how to manage and optimize these partnerships through AI-powered campaign systems—ensuring that every collaboration not only reaches the right audience but also achieves the right outcomes.

Marcus and Ari Team Up

Marcus had been working as a digital marketing manager for a mid-sized tech startup in Austin. His company, *VoltSync*, had developed an innovative portable power bank with solar-charging capability, but despite months of social media efforts, sales remained flat. His CEO wanted influencer partnerships, but Marcus knew from experience how messy that could be. The last campaign he ran took weeks just to find creators, and even then, only a few delivered solid results. Determined not to repeat the same mistake, he decided to test an AI discovery platform called *InfluenceVision.*

After creating an account, Marcus uploaded his campaign objectives: target audience, price range, tone of communication, and budget. The platform immediately began scanning data from millions of creators across social platforms. In less than five minutes, it generated a detailed report with 42 influencer recommendations—each ranked by *relevance score*, *predicted engagement value*, and *audience authenticity rating*. He could even see heat maps showing where the influencers' followers were located and which posts had generated the highest emotional response.

One name caught his attention: *TechWithAri*. She had 58,000 followers on TikTok and was known for her honest reviews of green technology. Her audience aligned perfectly with

VoltSync's target: environmentally conscious millennials who valued innovation and sustainability. The AI's predictive score estimated that a single sponsored video could produce a 12% engagement rate and a 6x return on ad spend. Marcus smiled—he had never seen numbers this specific before.

With one click, he used the platform's auto-outreach feature. The system drafted a personalized message that mentioned Ari's recent video on renewable gadgets and proposed a collaboration emphasizing VoltSync's portability and eco-efficiency. It even auto-generated a fair compensation estimate using market-rate data. Within 24 hours, Ari responded positively, intrigued by the AI-generated proposal that seemed to perfectly understand her audience.

Once the collaboration began, *InfluenceVision* tracked every metric in real time. The dashboard displayed engagement rates, comment sentiment, and geographic data as Ari's video gained traction. It predicted that engagement would peak on day three and recommended that Marcus repost highlights on Instagram using automated captions optimized by the AI's language model. The post went viral in less than 48 hours, doubling the company's follower count and generating a surge of web traffic.

Encouraged, Marcus expanded the campaign. The AI suggested two other influencers whose audiences overlapped less than 25% with Ari's—ensuring broader reach without duplication. One specialized in outdoor adventure gear, the other in eco-lifestyle products. Both were mid-tier creators with loyal audiences. Within weeks, VoltSync's brand awareness skyrocketed, and the product became a top seller in its category on Amazon.

When Marcus presented the campaign results to his CEO, he explained how AI-driven discovery had replaced manual research entirely. The system had not only found perfect matches but predicted performance with remarkable accuracy. His report showed engagement growth of 260%, ROI exceeding projections, and near-zero wasted ad spend. The CEO approved a larger annual budget for influencer marketing and promoted Marcus to Director of Growth Strategy.

Months later, when Marcus was invited to speak at a marketing conference, he summarized his experience with a simple insight: "AI didn't just help us find influencers—it helped us understand them." He explained how algorithms could read tone, measure trust, and detect fake engagement better than any human team could. The audience listened as he described how smart matching systems transformed influencer marketing from an art into a precise science.

As Marcus left the stage to a round of applause, he reflected on how much his role had evolved. Instead of wasting days on spreadsheets and manual searches, he now focused on creative storytelling and long-term brand strategy. AI handled the mechanics—he handled the vision. The balance between automation and creativity had given *VoltSync* an edge, and Marcus knew this was only the beginning of a new era where marketing intelligence wasn't just smart—it was predictive.

Chapter 3: Building AI-Powered Influencer Campaign Systems

Once influencers are identified and matched using AI discovery systems, the next stage is campaign execution — where strategy meets automation. Building an AI-powered influencer campaign system involves integrating multiple tools, workflows, and analytics processes to manage every step of the collaboration seamlessly. The purpose of such a system is not just to automate tasks but to optimize performance in real time, eliminate human error, and create a scalable, repeatable model for future campaigns.

At its core, an AI-powered influencer campaign system is a centralized ecosystem that connects influencer discovery, outreach, contract management, content planning, performance tracking, and reporting into one unified workflow. Traditional campaign management often required multiple disconnected tools: spreadsheets for budgets, email for communication, and separate dashboards for analytics. This fragmentation wasted time and created data silos. AI systems eliminate those inefficiencies by syncing all operations under one platform.

To build an effective campaign system, marketers first define the **campaign architecture**. This includes key objectives (brand awareness, sales conversion, audience growth), deliverables (posts, videos, stories, or blogs), timelines, and budget allocations. Once defined, AI tools take over the mechanical side — assigning deadlines, tracking influencer progress, and analyzing campaign health metrics in real time. Smart dashboards use predictive modeling to flag potential underperforming influencers early, allowing managers to reallocate budgets before the campaign concludes.

A strong campaign system depends on **data integration**. AI analytics platforms connect to social media APIs, e-commerce stores, CRMs, and website analytics tools to gather unified performance data. These integrations allow the system to attribute influencer activity directly to measurable outcomes such as website visits, sales conversions, and lead captures. This level of visibility makes influencer marketing accountable to the same standards as other paid media channels. When integrated with AI ad attribution models, marketers can track multi-touch conversions — showing how influencer engagement leads to purchases over days or weeks rather than instant clicks.

One of the most valuable features of AI campaign systems is **automated content scheduling and optimization**. Once content is approved, AI determines the best times to publish based on audience behavior and historical engagement trends.

It can even adjust the posting order dynamically to avoid audience fatigue. Some systems use reinforcement learning — a form of machine learning that continually tests and refines content delivery patterns for maximum engagement. This means campaigns evolve as they run, improving automatically with each iteration.

AI performance prediction is another cornerstone of these systems. Before content even goes live, AI models simulate potential outcomes based on visual style, caption tone, hashtag strategy, and historical post data. For example, the system might predict that an influencer's carousel post will achieve a 3.2% engagement rate while a 30-second video with similar messaging will reach 6.7%. Marketers can then adjust creative formats and messaging in advance rather than after a campaign underperforms. This predictive intelligence prevents waste and ensures content is data-informed from inception.

Campaign systems also rely heavily on **AI sentiment analysis**. By analyzing comments and audience reactions in real time, AI can identify whether a campaign is generating positive, neutral, or negative sentiment. If the tone begins to shift unfavorably — perhaps due to misunderstood messaging or backlash — the system alerts campaign managers instantly. This allows brands to respond quickly, adjust captions, or release clarifying posts before reputational damage spreads.

Another critical element is **AI-driven budgeting and forecasting**. Advanced systems allocate funds dynamically based on performance indicators. For instance, if one influencer's content is outperforming others by a significant margin, the system automatically increases their budget allocation or boosts promotion to capitalize on momentum. This approach mirrors programmatic advertising, where spending is continuously optimized for highest ROI. AI eliminates emotional decision-making by focusing purely on data-driven performance.

Building an AI campaign system also requires careful **human oversight**. While automation enhances efficiency, creativity and strategic judgment still depend on human input. AI provides insights — not intuition. Marketers must interpret data in context, considering nuances like brand tone, audience psychology, and cultural relevance. The most successful campaigns are hybrids where AI handles logistics and analytics while humans drive storytelling, empathy, and creative innovation.

To implement these systems effectively, teams often integrate tools like HypeAuditor, AspireIQ, Upfluence, and CreatorIQ for influencer management, combined with data platforms like Google Analytics, HubSpot, or Shopify for conversion tracking. These platforms can be connected through automation tools such as Zapier or Make.com to ensure seamless data flow. Once built, the result is a fully automated, continuously learning ecosystem that runs influencer marketing campaigns with precision, scalability, and transparency.

In essence, an AI-powered influencer campaign system transforms influencer marketing from a creative experiment into a predictable growth engine. It provides the structure, accountability, and optimization necessary to maximize results while minimizing manual work. By merging human creativity with AI automation, businesses can run more campaigns, manage more influencers, and achieve higher ROI — all without expanding their marketing teams. This is not the future of marketing; it is the new standard.

Jenna Takes Over

When Jenna took over as head of digital strategy for *BluePeak Apparel*, the brand was struggling. Their influencer campaigns were chaotic—too many creators, missed deadlines, inconsistent content, and unclear results. Every few months, the team would launch a new campaign only to repeat the same cycle: late posts, misaligned messaging, and unclear ROI. Jenna knew that if the company wanted to scale, it needed a complete system overhaul.

She began researching AI campaign management tools and discovered a platform called *PromoSync AI*. It promised to automate influencer selection, content scheduling, and performance tracking in one unified dashboard. Skeptical but curious, Jenna signed up for a trial and connected BluePeak's social accounts, Shopify store, and Google Analytics. Within minutes, the system populated with their existing influencer data, sorting it by performance metrics she had never seen before: *predicted engagement*, *audience overlap*, and *sentiment trendline*.

The transformation began immediately. Instead of manually emailing influencers, Jenna used the system's auto-outreach module, which personalized messages based on each creator's content style and history with the brand. Contracts were automatically generated using templates that included deliverables, posting schedules, and payment milestones. When influencers accepted, the platform synced with their content calendars and sent reminders automatically. For the first time, campaigns ran without constant follow-up.

Jenna set up her first AI-powered campaign — a spring launch featuring BluePeak's new eco-friendly activewear line. The AI analyzed historical sales data and determined that influencer posts featuring outdoor scenery performed 48% better than studio shots. It also predicted the ideal posting times for each influencer based on their audience's behavior. Instead of launching all content on the same day, the system staggered posts over ten days to maximize visibility and avoid saturation.

During the campaign, Jenna watched the dashboard in real time. The AI flagged which influencers were generating the highest conversions and which were underperforming. When one influencer's engagement dropped unexpectedly, the system alerted her that a recent algorithm change had affected reach. It suggested reallocating budget to a better-performing post and automatically boosted it as a paid ad extension. That single decision, made by AI in seconds, improved the campaign ROI by 28%.

Midway through the campaign, sentiment analysis detected an unusual spike in comments mentioning "sizing issues." The AI summarized the concern and provided a visual heatmap showing the posts where it appeared most frequently. Jenna's team immediately released a follow-up post clarifying sizing details and offering a discount code for exchanges. The proactive response prevented potential backlash and increased customer trust.

By the campaign's end, the numbers were staggering. Sales were up 310%, audience reach had doubled, and influencer collaboration costs dropped by nearly 40% thanks to automation. More impressively, Jenna's team—once overwhelmed by spreadsheets—now spent their time brainstorming creative ideas instead of chasing metrics. The AI handled everything else: performance prediction, budget allocation, and reporting.

A few weeks later, Jenna presented her results at the company's quarterly meeting. The CEO, impressed, asked how she had achieved such precision with a small team. She explained that PromoSync AI had essentially become a digital campaign manager—tracking, forecasting, and optimizing in real time. "The difference," she said, "is that AI doesn't just manage influencers; it manages outcomes."

Her words stuck with the leadership team. BluePeak quickly adopted AI automation across all marketing departments. What began as a test had become the company's most successful digital transformation project. Jenna's strategic vision—paired with AI's analytical power—had turned influencer marketing into a data-driven growth system that could run itself.

As she left the office that evening, Jenna reflected on how much had changed. Campaigns no longer felt like risks. Every decision was informed by data, every influencer collaboration tracked automatically, and every result connected directly to revenue. The chaos had turned into clarity. She realized that this was what the future of marketing looked like: intelligent systems working quietly in the background, allowing creative minds to focus on what they do best—telling stories that move people.

Chapter 4: Automating Influencer Outreach, Contracts, and Collaboration

The outreach and collaboration process has traditionally been one of the most time-intensive stages in influencer marketing. From writing personalized outreach emails to negotiating rates and tracking contract terms, it often required hours of manual effort for each partnership. As campaigns scaled, this became unsustainable. AI has completely reshaped this process by introducing automation systems capable of managing outreach, generating compliant contracts, and maintaining seamless communication with influencers across all campaign stages.

AI outreach automation begins with data-driven personalization. Instead of sending generic messages, AI systems analyze an influencer's recent content, engagement patterns, and brand tone to generate messages that sound authentic and relevant. These tools use natural language processing (NLP) to craft outreach templates that adapt automatically to each influencer's niche, style, and voice. For instance, an AI system reaching out to a travel vlogger might highlight how the brand aligns with the influencer's focus on adventure and sustainability, while for a tech reviewer, it would emphasize innovation and product quality. This level of contextual personalization increases response rates by up to 70% compared to manual outreach.

Once contact is initiated, **AI negotiation assistants** take over. These systems analyze historical compensation data, engagement rates, and influencer tiers to recommend fair and competitive offers. They can dynamically adjust proposed budgets based on performance predictions and influencer demand. This ensures that brands never overpay while influencers feel valued and fairly compensated. Some advanced tools even use predictive analytics to estimate the probability of acceptance at different price points, allowing marketers to fine-tune proposals in real time.

Contract automation is another critical advancement. Generating and managing contracts manually often led to delays and inconsistencies. AI-driven contract systems streamline the entire process by auto-generating legally compliant agreements based on selected campaign parameters—such as deliverables, deadlines, content usage rights, exclusivity clauses, and payment terms. These systems automatically populate influencer names, addresses, and compensation details, drastically reducing administrative workload. Additionally, integrated e-signature capabilities allow both parties to finalize agreements within minutes, enabling campaigns to launch faster and with greater accuracy.

AI also enhances **collaboration workflow management**. Once contracts are signed, collaboration dashboards powered by AI provide centralized communication and task tracking. Influencers can upload drafts, submit posts for approval, and receive real-time feedback. Meanwhile, AI monitors deadlines, sends automated reminders, and ensures deliverables stay on schedule. Predictive completion tracking helps managers forecast whether all campaign content will be delivered on time based on past behavior and engagement frequency. This proactive management approach eliminates bottlenecks before they occur.

A significant innovation in this phase is **AI compliance verification**. Every brand must ensure that sponsored posts meet disclosure and brand guidelines. AI tools automatically review influencer content before and after publication to confirm compliance with legal standards such as FTC disclosure rules ("#ad" or "#sponsored") and brand tone requirements. Using computer vision and text recognition, the AI can identify if posts include required hashtags, correct logo placement, or brand-approved phrasing. This prevents legal risk and ensures consistent brand representation across all influencer collaborations.

Another area where AI has made a major impact is **cross-team collaboration**. Large influencer programs often involve multiple departments—marketing, legal, finance, and customer support. AI collaboration hubs integrate these teams within a single platform. For example, legal teams receive automatic alerts when contracts are executed; finance departments are notified when influencer milestones are completed and payments are due. This real-time data synchronization eliminates miscommunication and keeps every stakeholder informed.

AI communication tools also foster stronger relationships between brands and influencers. Chatbots and automated assistants can provide 24/7 support, answering frequently asked questions about campaign terms, payment status, or creative briefs. These assistants are trained on brand-specific guidelines, ensuring that all responses remain consistent and professional. For influencers managing multiple collaborations simultaneously, this creates a smoother experience, encouraging long-term partnerships built on efficiency and reliability.

Moreover, **AI collaboration scoring systems** are emerging as a powerful tool for future campaign planning. After each campaign, the AI evaluates both brand and influencer performance metrics—timeliness, responsiveness, quality of content, and overall results. Each influencer receives a collaboration score that reflects their professionalism and impact. These scores feed back into discovery algorithms, allowing brands to prioritize top-performing influencers in future campaigns while filtering out unreliable partners.

By automating outreach, contracts, and collaboration, AI transforms what was once a disjointed process into an efficient, self-improving workflow. Campaign managers can focus on creative strategy and brand growth instead of repetitive administrative work. Most importantly, automation creates a better experience for both sides—brands achieve consistency and speed, while influencers enjoy clarity, fairness, and trust.

In this new ecosystem, influencer marketing becomes a system of collaboration rather than chaos. The fusion of AI negotiation, contract automation, and predictive collaboration ensures that campaigns move from concept to execution with precision, transparency, and accountability. As we progress to the next chapter, we'll explore how these automated collaborations feed directly into **AI-powered performance analytics and real-time optimization**, ensuring every campaign not only runs smoothly but delivers measurable success.

Carla Chooses CollabFlow AI

Carla worked as a marketing director for *EcoWave Electronics*, a company that produced solar-powered home gadgets. She had been in the industry long enough to remember when influencer outreach meant scrolling through social media for hours, copying email addresses, and sending dozens of cold messages that went unanswered. Each campaign felt like a maze of spreadsheets, messages, and contracts that never quite lined up. When her CEO announced the launch of their new smart solar lamp, she knew it was time to modernize her approach.

After researching automation tools, she chose *CollabFlow AI*, a system designed to manage influencer relationships end-to-end. As soon as she imported her target influencer list, the AI generated personalized outreach messages that read like they were written by a human social media manager. Each message referenced recent posts, complimented the influencer's creative style, and explained exactly how EcoWave's product aligned with their audience's interests. Carla was stunned — it felt personal, yet she hadn't written a single word herself.

Within a week, responses started flooding in. Out of 40 influencers contacted, 32 replied — an 80% response rate, something she'd never seen before. CollabFlow's negotiation assistant analyzed engagement data and suggested optimal compensation offers for each influencer. It even flagged one creator whose pricing was 35% higher than industry standards and recommended an adjusted offer likely to be accepted. Carla accepted the system's recommendation, and the influencer agreed the same day.

Once deals were finalized, CollabFlow generated digital contracts automatically. Carla watched as the system created customized agreements with clauses for exclusivity, deliverables, and content ownership — all compliant with FTC guidelines. Influencers signed electronically, and payments were scheduled automatically based on completion milestones. The entire process, which once took weeks, now happened in hours.

When campaign production began, the collaboration dashboard became Carla's control center. Each influencer had their own portal to upload drafts, submit posts, and communicate with the brand. The AI monitored submissions and sent polite reminders before deadlines approached. If an influencer posted without required hashtags, the system detected it instantly and issued an automated correction message. There were no awkward follow-ups or missed disclosures — everything stayed organized and compliant.

Halfway through the campaign, Carla received an AI alert: "Potential delay detected — influencer @SunnyTech has not posted in 72 hours." The system analyzed historical posting patterns and projected a 40% chance of missed deadline. Carla quickly sent a message through the platform, and the influencer responded that her camera had malfunctioned. Within minutes, the AI suggested reassigning part of the deliverable to another influencer with available bandwidth. The switch was seamless, and the campaign stayed on track.

By the end of the quarter, EcoWave's influencer marketing performance had more than doubled. The campaign generated 1.8 million impressions, 25,000 website visits, and a 34% increase in direct sales. But the best part was how stress-free it felt. Every influencer had clear instructions, every contract was automated, and every issue was resolved instantly.

Carla presented the results to the executive team with a slide titled "AI: Our New Marketing Assistant." She explained how CollabFlow handled 90% of her administrative workload, allowing her to focus on creative partnerships and storytelling. The CEO asked, half-jokingly, "So, when do we hire this AI full-time?" Carla smiled. "We already did — it just doesn't need a desk."

Months later, EcoWave's influencer program became a model for automation excellence. Influencers began recommending the brand to others because of how easy and professional the collaboration process was. Carla built long-term relationships with high-performing creators and scaled campaigns into international markets — all through a system that worked 24/7, never forgot a deadline, and never sent a message late.

As she looked at the final campaign dashboard summarizing the quarter's success, Carla reflected on how far marketing had evolved. Outreach wasn't about chasing influencers anymore; it was about attracting them with professionalism, data, and efficiency. AI had turned the process of negotiation, contracting, and collaboration into a smooth, intelligent workflow — and in doing so, it gave Carla the one thing every marketer dreams of: control without chaos.

Chapter 5: AI Analytics and Real-Time Campaign Optimization

Data has always been the backbone of successful marketing, but in influencer marketing, it was once difficult to obtain accurate, actionable insights. Brands could measure likes, comments, and impressions, but they couldn't truly understand *why* campaigns performed well or poorly. Artificial intelligence has changed that reality entirely. AI analytics and real-time optimization now allow marketers to measure campaign effectiveness at every stage, identify what drives conversions, and automatically adjust strategies while campaigns are still live. This chapter explores how these systems work and how to use them to maximize ROI and campaign predictability.

At its foundation, **AI analytics** in influencer marketing involves collecting, processing, and interpreting vast volumes of social and behavioral data. Modern platforms track more than just engagement; they analyze metrics such as audience sentiment, content virality potential, retention rates, and conversion pathways. By integrating data from social media APIs, e-commerce platforms, CRMs, and ad tracking systems, AI creates a complete performance picture that goes far beyond vanity metrics. Marketers can now see how every post contributes to brand awareness, lead generation, or direct revenue.

The next layer is **predictive analytics**. Traditional marketing looked backward; AI looks forward. Machine learning models trained on historical data can predict future outcomes with remarkable accuracy. They identify which influencers are likely to outperform based on current engagement patterns, which audiences are more likely to convert, and which creative assets will deliver the highest ROI. For instance, if AI detects that video content featuring behind-the-scenes brand stories generates 40% higher conversions than product-only visuals, it immediately recommends adjustments to upcoming posts. Predictive analytics transform campaigns into living systems that learn and improve continuously.

AI analytics platforms also provide **attribution modeling**—a long-standing challenge in influencer marketing. Determining exactly how an influencer's post leads to a sale was once nearly impossible, especially when users interacted with multiple touchpoints before purchasing. Now, AI uses multi-touch attribution models that assign weighted value to each interaction across the customer journey. For example, an influencer's Instagram reel may initiate brand awareness, while a YouTube review drives mid-funnel engagement, and a retargeting ad closes the sale. By analyzing patterns across all interactions, AI shows how influencers contribute to revenue both directly and indirectly.

Real-time optimization is where AI's capabilities truly shine. Once a campaign is live, the system constantly monitors performance metrics and compares them against predictive baselines. If engagement or conversion rates drop below expectations, AI automatically tests alternative variables — such as changing captions, adjusting posting times, or reallocating ad budgets. These micro-adjustments occur in real time without requiring manual intervention. The result is a campaign that evolves dynamically, always moving toward its highest-performing state.

Another major breakthrough is **AI-driven creative analysis**. Using computer vision and natural language processing, these systems can interpret both visuals and text to determine what type of content resonates best with audiences. They can identify patterns such as color palettes that attract higher engagement or phrasing styles that generate more comments. Over time, the AI learns each brand's unique engagement DNA and provides creative recommendations accordingly. This feedback loop ensures that every new campaign starts from a stronger, data-informed baseline.

Sentiment analysis continues to play a critical role in optimization. AI not only measures how many people engage with a post but how they *feel* about it. Advanced algorithms scan thousands of comments and messages, categorizing them as positive, neutral, or negative. If negative sentiment begins to rise, the system alerts managers and suggests strategic responses such as adjusting messaging tone or releasing follow-up content. This helps maintain brand reputation and ensures emotional resonance remains positive throughout the campaign.

AI reporting and visualization tools simplify complex data interpretation for decision-makers. Dashboards use visual storytelling to summarize performance across influencers, platforms, and time periods. Heat maps, predictive curves, and conversion funnels give an instant overview of where success is occurring and where improvements are needed. These dashboards can also generate executive summaries automatically, saving countless hours of manual reporting and allowing leadership to make faster, data-backed decisions.

One of the most impactful advantages of AI analytics is **adaptive budgeting**. Traditional budgets are static — determined before a campaign begins. AI, however, treats budgeting as dynamic. When one influencer's content performs exceptionally well, the system can automatically increase promotion or allocate paid ad support to amplify reach. Conversely, it can pause or reduce investment in underperforming segments. This dynamic resource reallocation maximizes efficiency and guarantees that budgets are always used in the most profitable way.

Finally, AI enables **benchmarking across industries and competitors**. Some systems aggregate anonymized data from thousands of campaigns to show how a brand's performance compares to others in the same category. This contextual insight reveals whether a campaign's engagement rate is average, above market, or outstanding. Over time, these benchmarks become strategic guides for setting realistic expectations and identifying new opportunities.

In summary, AI analytics and real-time optimization bring precision, adaptability, and intelligence to influencer marketing. Instead of waiting weeks for reports, brands now operate in a continuous feedback loop—measuring, learning, and improving daily. The ability to predict outcomes, optimize campaigns mid-flight, and visualize results instantly represents a fundamental shift in how marketing is managed. With AI, influencer marketing moves from subjective evaluation to objective, quantifiable success.

Luis Wants to Know Why Some Campaigns go Viral

When Luis joined *BrightFuel Nutrition* as digital marketing manager, he inherited a problem that nearly every brand faced: inconsistent influencer performance. Some collaborations drove major sales spikes, while others barely moved the needle. His reports looked like guesswork, and upper management demanded answers. "Why do some campaigns go viral while others disappear?" his director asked during a tense quarterly review. Luis didn't have an answer — yet.

Determined to fix the problem, he convinced his team to adopt an AI analytics platform called *InsightFlow*. The system promised predictive modeling, real-time optimization, and comprehensive attribution tracking for influencer campaigns. Once integrated, InsightFlow connected BrightFuel's Instagram, TikTok, YouTube, Shopify, and CRM data into a single dashboard. For the first time, Luis could see the entire funnel — from first impression to final purchase — in one place.

The next campaign featured five fitness influencers promoting BrightFuel's new pre-workout formula. As content rolled out, InsightFlow analyzed each post in real time. It measured not just engagement rates, but sentiment and conversion data. Within 24 hours, Luis noticed something remarkable: the AI detected that influencer *@FitAlex*'s videos had 45% higher retention and 2.3x more positive comments than average. The system recommended increasing budget allocation to boost those videos through paid amplification while pausing underperforming posts. Luis approved the change instantly.

By day three, conversions were already climbing. But the AI wasn't done. It flagged that one influencer's posts were generating unusually high click-throughs but low purchases. Drilling down, Luis discovered through sentiment analysis that many users commented they didn't understand the product's ingredients. The AI recommended creating a short explainer video addressing those concerns. Luis quickly coordinated with the influencer, who filmed a 30-second clip clarifying the science behind the supplement. The result? Conversion rates tripled within 48 hours.

Midway through the campaign, the dashboard displayed predictive graphs forecasting overall ROI. Based on real-time performance trends, InsightFlow predicted a 6.8x return on ad spend by the campaign's end — up from the original projection of 3.2x. The AI continued making micro-adjustments daily: optimizing posting times, testing new captions, and reallocating ad support based on each influencer's momentum. For Luis, it felt like having a team of analysts working around the clock.

As the campaign ended, InsightFlow automatically generated a 20-page report summarizing every metric: top-performing influencers, audience demographics, emotional engagement levels, and total revenue contribution. The data was presented in clean visuals with executive summaries already written. Luis didn't have to prepare a single slide. When he presented the results, his director was speechless — campaign revenue had surpassed goals by 240%.

The biggest revelation came from the attribution model. The AI showed that one influencer's early video, though not the highest in engagement, had driven over 40% of total conversions indirectly by creating awareness that later led to purchases through retargeting ads. This insight changed how the team valued influencers—not just by direct sales, but by their contribution across the customer journey.

A few months later, Luis was promoted to Head of Digital Strategy. In meetings with new clients, he often shared one key lesson: "AI doesn't replace marketers—it teaches them how to see patterns they couldn't see before." He described how real-time optimization had turned BrightFuel's influencer marketing into a self-improving machine, capable of predicting, adjusting, and outperforming every campaign before it even ended.

Today, when Luis logs into InsightFlow, he no longer wonders why some campaigns succeed and others fail. The answers are clear, the results are measurable, and the improvements are constant. Influencer marketing had finally evolved from guesswork into precision science.

Chapter 6: Predictive ROI, Budget Automation, and Smart Scaling

Once AI analytics establish a foundation for performance tracking and optimization, the next step in influencer marketing mastery is using **predictive ROI modeling** and **automated budgeting** to scale intelligently. In traditional marketing, ROI was calculated after campaigns ended, providing only retrospective insight. Today, artificial intelligence enables marketers to forecast profitability *before* launching campaigns, continuously optimize spending during execution, and automatically scale high-performing collaborations in real time. This evolution transforms influencer marketing from reactive to predictive – from experimentation to precision growth.

At the heart of predictive ROI is **machine learning modeling**. AI systems analyze thousands of data points from past campaigns—engagement rates, conversions, audience demographics, content types, and sentiment—to identify patterns that correlate with success. These models don't just calculate averages; they learn from nonlinear relationships, uncovering hidden variables such as how emotional tone in captions influences purchase behavior or how posting time impacts revenue by region. Once trained, these models can predict the expected return on investment for new influencer collaborations, sometimes with accuracy exceeding 90%.

Predictive ROI analysis enables **pre-campaign simulation**. Before committing any budget, marketers can input hypothetical variables—like influencer choice, platform, post format, and duration—and receive estimated performance ranges. For example, AI might predict that a mid-tier influencer on TikTok could generate a 5.6x ROI versus a top-tier Instagram creator expected to deliver only 2.8x ROI at double the cost. This allows for smarter decision-making, resource prioritization, and risk mitigation long before money is spent.

The next layer is **budget automation**—a dynamic allocation system driven by live campaign performance. Traditional budgeting is rigid, with predetermined amounts assigned to influencers, ads, and platforms. AI systems, however, treat budgets as fluid. When the algorithm detects that certain influencers or posts are outperforming projections, it automatically reallocates additional funds to boost those assets. Likewise, if certain segments underperform, the system reduces spending or pauses them entirely. This ensures every dollar contributes to maximum output in real time, without manual adjustments.

AI budgeting systems also optimize **cross-platform distribution**. They can assess performance differences between networks—Instagram, YouTube, TikTok, and X—and shift investment accordingly. For instance, if AI determines that YouTube influencer reviews are generating 65% of conversions while Instagram stories produce only 20%, the system automatically adjusts ad amplification toward YouTube. This level of precision replaces human bias with statistical accuracy, ensuring scaling decisions are always grounded in data, not instinct.

Another critical advancement is **lifetime value forecasting (LTV)**. Influencer marketing doesn't end at the first sale. Many customers engage repeatedly or become loyal advocates. AI tracks downstream customer behavior to calculate the long-term value generated by each influencer collaboration. A creator whose audience yields a smaller initial ROI may, over time, generate higher repeat-purchase value. Predictive systems account for these trends, helping marketers focus not only on short-term results but sustainable, compounding profitability.

Scaling campaigns intelligently also requires **AI clustering and segmentation**. By analyzing audience overlap and content performance, AI identifies which influencer groups produce synergistic effects. For instance, three mid-tier influencers with partially shared audiences may collectively outperform a single mega-influencer due to network amplification. The algorithm uses these insights to recommend optimal combinations of creators for maximum reach without redundancy. This enables marketers to scale horizontally—expanding with multiple complementary influencers—rather than vertically through a single expensive partnership.

AI predictive modeling also minimizes risk by identifying **budget thresholds and diminishing returns**. Beyond a certain point, increasing ad spend or influencer compensation doesn't proportionally increase ROI. Machine learning models forecast where that point lies, allowing brands to cap spending efficiently. This ensures profitability remains consistent, even as campaigns scale into larger markets or across multiple languages.

Smart scaling isn't just about spending more—it's about spending *smarter*. AI continuously evaluates when and where to scale. It measures momentum indicators such as engagement velocity, audience growth, and sentiment stability to determine the ideal time to expand reach or replicate campaigns. If the system predicts that a campaign has reached saturation—meaning new impressions no longer convert—it automatically recommends shifting focus to new influencers, creative formats, or geographic markets. Ultimately, predictive ROI and automated budgeting systems turn influencer marketing into an engine of compounding returns. Instead of isolated campaigns, brands operate continuous growth loops—testing, learning, and scaling in real time. This automation doesn't remove human strategy; it enhances it. Marketers gain deeper visibility, better control, and the freedom to focus on creativity while AI manages optimization and resource allocation in the background.

As brands adopt predictive modeling and smart scaling, the role of the marketing manager evolves from analyst to architect. No longer buried in spreadsheets, professionals can now forecast performance confidently, allocate budgets dynamically, and drive sustained growth through automation. This represents the pinnacle of AI influencer marketing — a self-optimizing ecosystem where campaigns predict their own success, budgets adjust automatically, and scaling becomes a science rather than a gamble.

Sophia The CMO

Sophia was the chief marketing officer at *PulseWear*, a growing fitness apparel brand that had gained moderate traction through influencer collaborations. Despite decent engagement, her campaigns lacked predictability. One influencer's posts would drive thousands of sales, while another's content with similar reach produced almost nothing. Each quarter felt like a gamble — some wins, some misses. What she wanted was control. What she found was *PredictIQ*, an AI system that promised to forecast ROI and automate budget scaling in real time.

Her first test came during the launch of PulseWear's new "SmartFit" leggings — embedded with biometric sensors that tracked calories and muscle activity. It was a bold innovation, and Sophia wanted precision. She uploaded a list of potential influencers into PredictIQ, entering campaign goals, pricing ranges, and creative formats. Within minutes, the platform simulated ROI projections for every possible collaboration. The results were eye-opening: the AI predicted that three mid-tier TikTok creators could generate a combined ROI of 7.4x — outperforming a single celebrity influencer who demanded five times the budget.

Guided by the data, Sophia approved the AI's plan. As soon as the campaign launched, PredictIQ began monitoring performance in real time. When one influencer's behind-the-scenes workout video gained 300% higher engagement than expected, the AI automatically reallocated additional budget to promote it as a paid ad across multiple platforms. Conversely, it detected another influencer's story sequence was underperforming and cut funding instantly. This automated budget balancing saved Sophia's team hours of analysis and boosted total ROI mid-campaign.

Midway through the campaign, PredictIQ's predictive model updated its forecast, projecting that overall ROI could reach 9.2x if additional content was released by a specific date. The AI detected a trend in audience behavior — engagement peaked on Thursdays between 6:00 and 9:00 PM. Sophia acted quickly, commissioning the top-performing influencers to post fresh content within that window. The result was a viral surge that pushed sales to record highs.

But PredictIQ's insights didn't stop at short-term results. It also tracked post-campaign customer retention. The AI identified that followers from one influencer, @ActiveLena, exhibited 40% higher repeat purchase rates. By calculating customer lifetime value, the system showed that Lena's audience, although smaller, was more profitable long term. Sophia decided to form an exclusive partnership with her, expanding future campaigns around that loyal demographic.

By the campaign's conclusion, PulseWear's revenue had increased by 220%, with marketing spend down 30% compared to the previous quarter. The AI-generated final report detailed every optimization made — budget reallocations, performance triggers, and LTV projections.

Sophia was impressed by one particular graph: a "profit prediction curve" that showed how PredictIQ had prevented overspending by pausing investments precisely when diminishing returns began. No human analyst could have reacted that quickly.

At the next board meeting, Sophia presented her findings. "We didn't just run a campaign," she said. "We ran a self-learning growth engine." She explained how PredictIQ continuously optimized ROI, managed budget flow, and scaled influencer partnerships without guesswork. The board members were astonished. One investor asked, "So what happens if the AI gets it wrong?" Sophia smiled. "It learns faster than we ever could."

Months later, PulseWear expanded globally using PredictIQ's forecasting data to plan launches in Europe and Asia. The system adjusted for currency variations, local engagement patterns, and cultural preferences automatically. What began as an experiment had evolved into a global scaling strategy fueled by predictive intelligence.

Standing in her office one evening, Sophia watched as the dashboard displayed a new alert: "Opportunity Detected — Influencer @FitTechMax trending in Germany, predicted ROI: 8.6x." Without hesitation, she clicked *Approve Collaboration.*

The system generated the proposal, budget plan, and contract instantly. The future of influencer marketing was no longer reactive — it was anticipatory.

Sophia realized she wasn't managing campaigns anymore; she was orchestrating a living, breathing system that grew smarter with every decision. PulseWear's marketing was now an organism that predicted success before it happened — proof that with AI, scaling wasn't just faster. It was inevitable.

Chapter 7: AI-Driven Content Intelligence and Creative Optimization

While audience targeting and budgeting are crucial, the true power of influencer marketing lies in content — the stories, visuals, and messages that connect emotionally with viewers. For years, creativity was considered an intuitive process that couldn't be quantified or automated. Today, that belief has been overturned. With artificial intelligence, brands can now analyze creative elements scientifically, predict which visuals and captions will perform best, and continuously optimize content based on real-time audience feedback. This process, known as **AI-driven content intelligence**, merges data analytics with creativity, producing content that feels authentic while achieving measurable impact.

At its core, AI-driven content intelligence involves analyzing every element of influencer-generated content — text, imagery, sound, tone, and structure — to identify what resonates most with target audiences. Machine learning models trained on millions of posts can determine how color schemes, emotional tone, or storytelling format influence engagement. For example, AI can detect that a product post featuring natural lighting and minimal text outperforms highly edited studio images by 38%. These insights allow marketers and influencers to create data-informed content without sacrificing authenticity.

One of the foundational technologies behind this evolution is **computer vision**. By scanning visual content, AI systems can identify patterns invisible to the human eye: color composition, object placement, facial expressions, and brand visibility. This technology can determine which aesthetic elements generate the highest engagement across categories. For instance, a fitness brand may learn that videos filmed outdoors with motion and natural light outperform gym-based content. These findings help shape creative direction before production begins, reducing trial and error and saving both time and budget.

Equally important is **natural language processing (NLP)**, which allows AI to evaluate captions, hashtags, and voiceovers. AI models analyze linguistic tone, emotional cues, and sentence structure to predict which styles attract more engagement. For example, captions that express personal experiences or use conversational tones tend to create higher comment activity than purely promotional text. NLP also enables **tone consistency analysis**, ensuring that influencer content aligns with a brand's desired messaging style — whether aspirational, educational, or humorous.

AI content intelligence platforms go beyond analysis; they also **generate creative recommendations**. Using predictive analytics, they can suggest ideal visual formats, posting styles, or even AI-generated templates optimized for each platform. Some systems, like Cortex or Pattern89, simulate how different creative combinations would perform and score them before launch. This allows teams to A/B test creative concepts virtually — before spending a dollar on production. The outcome is a creative workflow that is faster, smarter, and guided by data rather than intuition alone.

Another major development is **real-time creative optimization**. Once influencer content is published, AI tracks audience reactions across demographics, time zones, and devices. If the system detects declining engagement or negative sentiment, it immediately recommends changes — such as switching thumbnail images, modifying captions, or adjusting video duration. For video platforms like YouTube and TikTok, AI can even suggest re-editing segments based on viewer drop-off rates, ensuring that future uploads maintain maximum attention.

AI is also revolutionizing **brand alignment and compliance monitoring**. Algorithms can automatically scan influencer posts to confirm that logos, product placements, and messaging follow brand standards. Using image recognition, the system identifies whether a logo is clearly visible, whether the influencer adhered to product display requirements, and whether text overlays meet accessibility standards. This automated review process maintains consistency across hundreds of influencer posts without requiring manual checks.

For global brands, AI content intelligence helps adapt creative assets for different cultural contexts. By analyzing language nuances, visual symbolism, and regional engagement trends, AI ensures that campaigns remain locally relevant while maintaining brand integrity. For instance, a gesture or color that resonates in the U.S. might carry a different meaning in Asia. AI localization engines analyze those cultural variables and recommend content adjustments to avoid misinterpretation.

The creative optimization process doesn't replace human artistry — it amplifies it. AI provides the data foundation that informs creativity, giving marketers confidence that their ideas are supported by insight, not guesswork. Influencers retain their voice and authenticity, but they are guided by intelligent feedback that enhances performance. The collaboration between human creativity and AI precision produces a balance of originality and reliability rarely achievable in traditional marketing.

Ultimately, AI-driven content intelligence closes the gap between data and creativity. It transforms content creation into a measurable, iterative process — one where every creative decision contributes to predictable results. The ability to test, analyze, and optimize continuously ensures that brands never fall behind trends or audience expectations. By understanding not just *what* content performs but *why* it performs, marketers unlock a new era of scalable creativity — intelligent, data-backed, and emotionally resonant.

The AI Knows My Audience

Ava had always prided herself on her creative instincts. As a senior brand manager for *GlowTheory Cosmetics*, she believed good marketing was about emotion — color, music, energy, and message. But lately, her campaigns felt unpredictable. Some influencer videos went viral for reasons she couldn't explain, while others—equally beautiful—barely gained traction. When her CEO introduced an AI tool called *VisionPulse*, promising data-driven creativity, she was skeptical. "You can't teach algorithms emotion," she said. Still, she agreed to try it for the company's new skincare launch.

She began by uploading dozens of influencer videos, captions, and images from previous campaigns into VisionPulse. The system began analyzing them instantly. Within minutes, it displayed a visual heatmap of what caught viewers' attention first — faces, lighting, and motion. Then came the insights: videos with natural daylight outperformed studio shots by 42%. Captions that started with personal stories had double the engagement of those with direct product pitches. And pastel color palettes triggered more positive sentiment than bold reds or blacks. Ava was astonished. "It's like the AI knows my audience better than I do," she admitted.

Armed with this knowledge, Ava restructured her influencer brief. She instructed creators to film outdoors, use storytelling captions, and highlight authenticity over perfection. VisionPulse even suggested the ideal video length (23–30 seconds) and recommended avoiding overlaid text longer than six words. When the campaign launched, the AI monitored performance in real time. As engagement data rolled in, it began making micro-adjustments automatically — suggesting new hashtags, trimming underperforming clips, and even changing thumbnail images based on click-through trends.

Halfway through the campaign, Ava received an alert: "Engagement plateau detected. Recommendation: shift focus to morning skincare routines." The AI had noticed that posts about nighttime routines were saturating the feed, while audience interest was rising around morning rituals. Within 24 hours, Ava coordinated with three influencers to post new content featuring sunrise scenes and daily-use products.

Engagement rebounded immediately, exceeding previous peaks by 37%.

But what impressed Ava most was how the AI handled localization. GlowTheory was expanding into Latin America, and VisionPulse analyzed linguistic sentiment across Spanish captions. It identified that the phrase "piel perfecta" ("perfect skin") was less relatable in that market than "piel saludable" ("healthy skin"), which evoked authenticity and self-care. Adjusting that single phrase improved engagement by 54% in Spanish-speaking regions.

At campaign's end, the AI-generated report compared every creative element — lighting, tone, caption length, and visual style — showing which combinations produced the highest ROI. It even displayed a "creative DNA map," illustrating the unique characteristics shared by all top-performing posts. For the first time, creativity had become measurable.

When Ava presented the results at the company's strategy meeting, she said, "AI didn't replace our creativity — it refined it." Her team nodded, seeing how VisionPulse had transformed guesswork into precision. Instead of arguing over design preferences, they now made creative decisions backed by data. The AI had given them the confidence to innovate intelligently.

Months later, GlowTheory's campaigns were setting benchmarks across the beauty industry. Competitors noticed their consistency and engagement rates but couldn't replicate them without understanding the invisible advantage of AI-powered creative optimization. As Ava reviewed her dashboard late one night, she smiled at a new insight appearing on-screen: "Upcoming trend detected — minimalistic textures increasing engagement by 26%."

She whispered to herself, "The AI doesn't feel emotions, but it understands them." That realization marked a turning point. Ava no longer saw AI as a threat to creativity but as its most powerful ally — a silent partner ensuring that every story told reached its full potential.

Chapter 8: Automated Influencer Relationship Management and Long-Term Retention Systems

Influencer marketing doesn't end when a campaign concludes — in many ways, that's when the most valuable phase begins. Building and sustaining long-term relationships with influencers is one of the most powerful growth levers for brands. Repeat collaborations reduce onboarding costs, maintain message consistency, and deepen audience trust. Yet managing dozens or even hundreds of influencer relationships manually can be overwhelming. Artificial intelligence now provides a scalable solution through **automated influencer relationship management (IRM)** and retention systems designed to nurture long-term loyalty, performance consistency, and mutual growth.

The traditional approach to relationship management relied heavily on personal outreach and manual tracking. Spreadsheets were used to record contact details, campaign history, and payment status. Communication happened through fragmented emails, and follow-ups were often forgotten once a campaign ended. This lack of structure led to lost opportunities, inconsistent communication, and influencers drifting toward competitors. AI-driven IRM systems eliminate these inefficiencies by creating an intelligent, automated framework for communication, engagement, and performance analysis.

At the foundation of automated IRM is a **centralized influencer database** powered by AI. Every influencer interaction—emails, messages, campaign results, and payment records—is automatically captured and organized. The system builds detailed influencer profiles, complete with engagement history, audience analytics, preferred collaboration types, and sentiment trends. This allows brands to segment influencers not just by size or platform, but by performance reliability, creative style, and brand alignment. Instead of reactive management, marketers can proactively identify who to retain, re-engage, or upgrade to ambassador status.

AI plays a critical role in **relationship nurturing**. Through automated communication workflows, influencers receive personalized messages, performance summaries, and collaboration invitations tailored to their preferences. Natural language generation (NLG) tools craft messages that sound human, maintaining warmth and professionalism while ensuring consistency. These systems can automatically send thank-you notes after campaigns, share performance analytics, or offer future opportunities based on past results. This level of personalization builds trust and strengthens relationships at scale.

Predictive retention modeling is another transformative feature. AI analyzes behavioral data—such as response time, engagement quality, and collaboration frequency—to predict which influencers are most likely to continue working with the brand. It also identifies at-risk partners showing signs of disengagement, such as declining performance or delayed responses. The system then triggers alerts or personalized re-engagement strategies, such as offering performance-based bonuses, early product access, or exclusive ambassador programs. This proactive approach ensures valuable relationships aren't lost due to oversight.

Automation also enhances **influencer rewards and loyalty systems**. AI can manage tiered incentive programs similar to customer loyalty structures. Influencers who consistently deliver results move into higher tiers that unlock perks like increased compensation rates, co-branding opportunities, or early access to campaigns. Machine learning algorithms track progress automatically and update reward statuses in real time. These systems encourage long-term commitment and make influencers feel recognized as integral brand partners rather than temporary contractors. **Performance benchmarking** within IRM platforms adds further intelligence. AI continuously evaluates each influencer's performance across campaigns, comparing results against peers and market averages. Influencers receive automated scorecards summarizing their strengths and areas for improvement. This data empowers both parties—brands can refine collaborations strategically, and influencers can improve content quality using clear, objective feedback. Over time, this fosters mutual growth and higher-quality partnerships.

AI also enhances transparency and professionalism in financial management. Automated payment systems trigger disbursements based on verified deliverable completion and performance milestones. Smart contracts built on blockchain technology ensure that both influencer and brand obligations are fulfilled automatically, eliminating disputes. Payment histories and earnings analytics help influencers track income trends, while brands gain insights into cost efficiency and profitability per partner.

Finally, **AI-powered community engagement dashboards** allow brands to turn their influencer network into a thriving ecosystem. The system tracks collaboration overlaps, shared audiences, and co-engagement opportunities, recommending potential cross-collaborations between creators. This interconnected structure not only builds community but multiplies reach through synergistic partnerships. As networks grow, AI identifies "hub influencers" — creators whose relationships influence others — and recommends exclusive ambassador programs for them.

The long-term value of AI-driven IRM lies in sustainability. Rather than constantly chasing new creators, brands develop a stable ecosystem of loyal partners who understand their message and consistently deliver results. AI handles the operational workload, leaving human marketers to focus on creativity and relationship building. The outcome is a balanced system — efficient, personal, and scalable — that turns one-time influencers into lifelong brand advocates.

EcoSpark and Nathan

When Nathan joined *EcoSpark Home Goods* as partnership director, he inherited a massive spreadsheet with over 300 influencer contacts. The file was messy—duplicates, outdated emails, incomplete notes, and no record of who had performed well. Every campaign required starting over: reintroducing the brand, renegotiating rates, and retraining influencers on content expectations. Despite solid short-term results, EcoSpark struggled to build a consistent community of brand advocates. Nathan realized they weren't managing relationships—they were managing transactions.

To solve this, he introduced *RelateIQ*, an AI-powered influencer relationship management system. After uploading years of campaign data, RelateIQ automatically built detailed profiles for every influencer—organizing them by niche, audience demographics, reliability score, and sentiment analysis from past campaigns. Within minutes, Nathan could see who had driven the highest ROI, who had declined in engagement, and which partnerships had the most long-term potential.

The transformation began immediately. RelateIQ's automation engine sent personalized thank-you messages to every influencer who had worked with EcoSpark in the past 12 months. Each message included a mini performance report highlighting their results and inviting them to join the brand's new loyalty program. Influencers were impressed. One replied, "I've never seen a brand share data like this—it makes me feel like a real partner."

Next, Nathan implemented a **tiered reward system** powered by AI. Influencers were grouped into three categories: Silver, Gold, and Platinum. The AI automatically moved them between tiers based on performance metrics like engagement rate, on-time delivery, and sales impact. Platinum members received early product access and co-branded campaign opportunities. Gold members earned bonuses for exceeding targets. Silver members received growth tips generated by AI, helping them improve for future collaborations. Over time,

RelateIQ began predicting which influencers were likely to disengage. One alert notified Nathan that a creator, *@EcoLivingEmma*, had shown declining response times and reduced engagement. The system suggested a personalized outreach email offering early access to EcoSpark's new eco-cleaning product line. Emma accepted immediately, sharing that she had felt overlooked and was grateful for the exclusive opportunity. Her next campaign became one of the brand's top performers that quarter.

Financial automation brought further relief. Payments, once delayed for weeks, now processed automatically after deliverable verification. Smart contracts ensured both sides met obligations before funds released. Influencers appreciated the transparency, and disputes virtually disappeared. As trust grew, EcoSpark's influencer retention rate jumped from 48% to 87% in just six months.

The biggest breakthrough came when the AI began suggesting **collaborative opportunities** among influencers. RelateIQ identified creators with overlapping audiences and recommended joint campaigns. One collaboration between two sustainability influencers led to a viral cross-platform challenge that tripled engagement across both accounts. The system even tracked mutual followers gained from these partnerships, proving the compounded network effect. By the end of the year, EcoSpark had transformed from a brand chasing influencers into a community-led movement. Their top 50 creators formed a private ambassador network managed entirely through RelateIQ's dashboard. Campaigns ran smoother, messages stayed consistent, and audiences began recognizing EcoSpark as a household name in sustainable living.

During the company's annual review, the CEO asked Nathan what had made the biggest difference. He replied, "We stopped managing influencers like numbers and started nurturing them like partners — AI just gave us the tools to do it at scale."

Months later, as Nathan reviewed a dashboard showing dozens of active collaborations running simultaneously across multiple countries, he realized something profound: automation hadn't replaced relationships—it had *protected* them. The system handled reminders, data, and payments, while he focused on appreciation, communication, and creative alignment.

EcoSpark's influencer community was no longer a list of contacts; it was a living ecosystem. Each collaboration built upon the last, supported by a network that learned, adapted, and grew. AI had made it possible to turn fleeting partnerships into enduring brand loyalty — and in doing so, Nathan had built not just a marketing program, but a legacy of connection powered by intelligence.

Chapter 9: AI Security, Compliance, and Ethical Influencer Marketing

As artificial intelligence takes on a greater role in influencer marketing, new challenges emerge around **data security, compliance, and ethical responsibility**. The same tools that automate, optimize, and predict also handle massive volumes of sensitive data—audience analytics, private influencer information, and proprietary brand metrics. Without proper safeguards, this data can be exposed, misused, or even manipulated. AI-driven influencer marketing demands not only technical excellence but also ethical discipline. This chapter explores the frameworks, risks, and best practices that ensure every campaign operates securely, transparently, and responsibly.

The first pillar of ethical AI influencer marketing is **data privacy and security**. AI systems collect information from multiple sources: social media APIs, analytics dashboards, and influencer contracts. These datasets often include identifiable information such as email addresses, location data, and payment records. To remain compliant with global data protection regulations—like the GDPR (Europe), CCPA (California), and LGPD (Brazil)—brands must adopt strict data governance policies. This includes encrypting stored data, anonymizing personal identifiers, and limiting access to authorized personnel only. AI models used in influencer marketing should be trained on secure, anonymized datasets to prevent accidental leaks or misuse.

A critical aspect of compliance involves **consent management**. Influencers and consumers must clearly understand how their data is being used, stored, and analyzed. Brands should disclose when AI tools are being employed to evaluate engagement or sentiment. Consent should never be implied—it must be explicit and revocable. Ethical AI marketing platforms now include consent-tracking modules that record when and how data permissions were granted. These systems ensure compliance audits can be passed easily while protecting the integrity of all stakeholders involved.

The second pillar is **algorithmic transparency and bias mitigation**. AI algorithms are only as fair as the data they are trained on. If an AI discovery tool disproportionately recommends influencers from certain demographics while underrepresenting others, it perpetuates bias. Ethical marketers must regularly audit their algorithms to identify and correct patterns of discrimination. Using diverse training data, testing for representational fairness, and implementing explainable AI (XAI) frameworks allow brands to understand how and why specific influencers are selected or ranked.

Transparency is not optional—it is a fundamental requirement for trust.

Ethical influencer marketing also extends to **disclosure and authenticity**. Audiences have the right to know when they are viewing sponsored content. AI monitoring tools can automatically detect missing disclosures and prompt influencers to include them before posting. This protects both brands and creators from regulatory penalties. Ethical compliance also means avoiding deepfake content, manipulated endorsements, or AI-generated influencers that deceive audiences. While synthetic media can be a legitimate creative tool, it must be clearly labeled to maintain audience trust.

Another important dimension is **brand safety and content integrity**. AI content monitoring systems continuously scan influencer posts for potentially harmful or non-compliant material—such as offensive language, misinformation, or unapproved brand mentions. These systems use natural language understanding (NLU) and image recognition to flag violations instantly. Maintaining brand safety is not just about protecting reputation; it's about ensuring that partnerships align with company values and societal standards.

Financial transparency also falls under the ethical umbrella.

Automated payment systems should provide influencers with clear, traceable earnings records. Smart contracts ensure timely payments and mutual accountability. Brands that use AI for financial transactions must ensure compliance with anti-money-laundering (AML) and tax reporting laws. These measures reinforce professional integrity and sustain long-term trust within the influencer ecosystem.

As AI continues to evolve, **ethical governance frameworks** will become the backbone of sustainable marketing operations. Leading organizations are establishing internal AI ethics boards that review data use policies, algorithm updates, and automation practices. These boards include marketing experts, data scientists, and legal advisors who ensure compliance aligns with human values. The future of AI marketing will depend not only on innovation but on responsibility—the ability to create systems that serve people, not just profits.

Finally, true ethical AI influencer marketing embraces the principle of **human oversight**. AI should assist in decision-making, not replace it entirely. While automation manages data and processes efficiently, human judgment remains essential for understanding cultural nuances, emotional tone, and moral implications. The balance between

AI precision and human empathy ensures that marketing remains both effective and ethical.

When brands combine security, compliance, and transparency with intelligent automation, they build not only profitable campaigns but lasting credibility. Trust, once earned, becomes a competitive advantage that no algorithm can manufacture. The most advanced AI influencer marketing systems will not be those that automate the most tasks—but those that uphold the highest ethical standards while doing so.

Maya Address Algorithmic Bias

Maya had built her digital agency, *ClearView Strategies*, on innovation. Her team managed influencer campaigns for global clients across tech, fashion, and lifestyle industries. With dozens of AI tools powering everything from influencer discovery to predictive analytics, results were better than ever — but so was the risk. One morning, her legal director burst into her office holding a news article. A rival agency had suffered a data breach exposing hundreds of influencer contracts, including payment details and personal addresses. The fallout was devastating. Maya knew it could have been them.

That day, she made a decision: *ClearView* would become the model for ethical AI influencer marketing. Her first step was implementing an AI data governance system called *TrustLayer*. It encrypted every file, anonymized influencer identifiers, and restricted access based on roles. Even the AI models that analyzed engagement data used synthetic, privacy-protected versions of real information. Maya's legal team reviewed compliance under GDPR, CCPA, and international standards. "No influencer should ever have to worry about how their data is used," she told her staff.

Next, Maya addressed **algorithmic bias**. TrustLayer's analytics had shown that 68% of influencer recommendations came from English-speaking regions, unintentionally excluding valuable creators in Latin America and Southeast Asia. Working with her AI engineers, she retrained the recommendation model using multilingual and multicultural datasets. The following month, diversity in campaign selection improved dramatically. Clients noticed that their global reach and authenticity had expanded — not because of luck, but because of ethical intelligence.

Maya also focused on **transparency**. Every influencer who worked with ClearView received a data disclosure statement explaining what metrics were tracked, how AI was used, and how their information was protected. They could revoke consent at any time. Surprisingly, this openness increased trust and collaboration. One influencer wrote, "It's rare for an agency to treat creators like partners instead of data points."

During one major campaign for a beauty brand, the AI compliance monitor flagged missing disclosure tags on an influencer's post before it went live. Maya's team was able to fix it immediately, avoiding potential fines from regulators. The system also identified subtle issues, such as incomplete brand mentions and inaccessible image captions — helping the brand maintain full compliance while promoting inclusion for visually impaired audiences.

A few months later, a major client proposed using an AI-generated influencer avatar for their next campaign. The digital model looked human but wasn't. Maya hesitated. While the concept was technologically impressive, she insisted that the campaign clearly label the avatar as AI-generated. "We can innovate without deceiving," she explained. The client agreed, and the campaign became a success precisely because of its honesty. Audiences praised the brand for being transparent about the use of virtual technology.

Behind the scenes, ClearView also upgraded its payment system with blockchain-based smart contracts. Influencers were paid automatically after deliverables were verified by AI. Payments were traceable, secure, and instant — eliminating late fees and disputes. Transparency became the agency's calling card. Clients loved the efficiency; influencers loved the fairness.

By year's end, ClearView had achieved what few agencies could: 100% compliance with global data privacy laws and zero security incidents. Maya was invited to speak at an international marketing conference about "Ethical AI in Influencer Campaigns." She told the audience, "The future of AI in marketing isn't about what machines *can* do. It's about what they *should* do."

As applause filled the room, Maya realized that ethics had become her agency's competitive advantage. Clients didn't just hire *ClearView* for their AI systems—they hired them for their integrity. Every campaign they launched carried a reputation for safety, fairness, and transparency.

Months later, when a journalist asked Maya why she invested so heavily in compliance instead of focusing solely on profits, she replied, "Because trust is the only currency that compounds forever."

Her words captured the spirit of the new era. In a world driven by algorithms, it was the brands and marketers who upheld ethics and transparency that would stand the test of time. AI could predict clicks and optimize budgets—but only integrity could sustain influence.

Chapter 10: The Future of AI Influencer Marketing: Integration, Innovation, and Human–AI Collaboration

Artificial intelligence has already revolutionized influencer marketing — from discovery to analytics, from automation to compliance. But the real transformation lies ahead. The next generation of AI will not just assist marketers; it will integrate across every touchpoint of digital communication, enabling a fully connected marketing ecosystem where creativity, authenticity, and intelligence operate in harmony. This chapter explores what that future looks like — how integration, innovation, and human–AI collaboration will redefine how brands and influencers create, scale, and sustain influence.

The future begins with **total integration**. Today's influencer marketing systems already connect discovery tools, CRMs, analytics dashboards, and ad platforms. Tomorrow's systems will merge them into unified, AI-driven ecosystems. Campaigns will flow automatically from ideation to execution. When a brand launches a new product, AI will instantly identify relevant influencers, generate personalized briefs, predict ROI, schedule content, and track performance across every platform. These self-operating ecosystems will manage millions of interactions simultaneously while maintaining brand tone and consistency through AI-trained governance systems.

Integration will extend beyond marketing departments. Influencer data will merge with **sales forecasting, customer support, and product development**. For example, AI may analyze influencer campaign feedback to identify common product improvement suggestions. Customer sentiment collected through influencer comments will feed directly into R&D, enabling faster innovation cycles. AI won't just connect platforms — it will connect entire business functions, making influencer marketing a strategic pillar of organizational intelligence.

A second major shift will be the rise of **multimodal AI** — systems capable of understanding and generating text, images, video, audio, and even virtual environments simultaneously. These tools will transform how campaigns are conceptualized and delivered. Marketers will use simple voice prompts or natural language descriptions to create complete influencer campaign packages, including visuals, captions, and performance projections. Influencers will use the same technology to generate creative content faster, supported by AI co-creators that enhance rather than replace their personal style.

AI avatars and virtual influencers will evolve as well, but transparency and ethics will guide their use. Instead of replacing human creators, AI-generated personalities will supplement human campaigns by filling content gaps, localizing messaging for global markets, or providing 24/7 brand representation. The most advanced models will blend seamlessly with real influencers, creating hybrid ecosystems where authenticity and automation coexist.

The third wave of innovation will be **contextual personalization at scale**. AI will not only understand audience demographics but individual behaviors, emotions, and micro-moments. Real-time mood detection through sentiment and engagement patterns will enable influencers to adapt messaging dynamically. For example, if AI detects rising interest in eco-conscious content among an influencer's followers, it will recommend relevant products or adjust tone to emphasize sustainability. Marketing will evolve from mass communication to individualized conversation — intelligent, adaptive, and emotionally aware.

Emerging technologies will also empower **AI-powered co-creation between humans and machines**. Influencers will collaborate with generative AI tools that write scripts, design visuals, and even compose background music in real time. These tools will analyze each influencer's voice, pacing, and brand style to ensure every piece of content feels authentic. Human creativity will set direction, while AI provides speed, optimization, and scale. The result will be a new era of creative partnership — not human vs. machine, but human + machine.

Data ethics and transparency will remain at the center of this evolution. Future systems will include embedded **AI ethics engines** that automatically enforce compliance, track data lineage, and audit algorithmic fairness. Regulators will require brands to prove accountability for AI decisions, and certification programs will emerge for responsible AI marketing practices. In this environment, trust will become an asset as valuable as technology itself. Brands that combine intelligence with integrity will dominate the global landscape.

Finally, **AI education and skill evolution** will redefine professional marketing roles. The most successful marketers will no longer be those who manually execute tasks but those who design intelligent systems, interpret insights, and orchestrate automation. Influencers will learn to use AI tools as creative partners — mastering prompt design, generative storytelling, and predictive analytics. Human skills like empathy, strategic thinking, and emotional intelligence will become even more valuable, complementing AI's precision and scale.

In summary, the future of AI influencer marketing is not just about efficiency — it's about *elevation*. Integrated systems will unify the creative, analytical, and operational sides of marketing. Innovation will push boundaries with multimodal AI and adaptive personalization. And collaboration between humans and machines will give rise to campaigns that are not only intelligent but deeply human. The future belongs to brands and creators who embrace AI not as a replacement for creativity, but as a multiplier of it.

The Custom Creative Plan Generated by AI

In 2030, influencer marketing didn't look anything like it had a decade earlier. Campaigns that once required entire teams now ran autonomously through AI ecosystems that could plan, execute, and optimize in real time. For *NovaBlend,* a global wellness brand, this future had already arrived.

Elena, the company's marketing director, began her day by opening *HoloConnect AI,* a fully integrated marketing platform that managed all influencer campaigns across continents. The system greeted her with a summary: *"Three campaigns launched overnight. ROI projections updated. Sentiment analysis positive in 92% of regions."* The AI voice assistant, named *Atlas,* spoke in calm precision, its tone familiar yet reassuring. She reviewed the "Global Balance" campaign, where AI had already selected influencers, created personalized content packages, and even scheduled posts optimized for each time zone. Each influencer had a custom creative plan generated by AI — including pre-written captions, video scripts, and thumbnail templates based on their audience's engagement DNA. Elena hadn't written a single email. The system handled everything, yet every campaign still felt personal and authentic.

When a surge of engagement came from India, Atlas instantly adjusted. It localized captions into Hindi, Bengali, and Tamil using real-time translation and sentiment calibration, ensuring tone remained warm and genuine. In less than ten minutes, the localized campaign went live. Elena smiled. "We couldn't have done that in a week back in 2024," she thought.

Meanwhile, influencers worked with AI creative companions — virtual editors that suggested camera angles, adjusted lighting, and optimized pacing during recording. One influencer, *Ravi*, filmed a wellness vlog while his AI co-director, *Luna*, displayed real-time feedback in his glasses: *"Increase brightness by 10%. Smile more during product intro. Engagement projection: +12%."* It was seamless collaboration — human expression enhanced by AI precision.

Back at NovaBlend's headquarters, Elena attended the daily integration meeting — a holographic conference where AI summarized cross-department insights. Product R&D received feedback from influencer comments about flavor preferences; logistics adjusted distribution to match trending regions; customer service used sentiment data to preempt complaints. Influencer marketing had become the central nervous system of the company — feeding intelligence to every function.

But even in this hyper-automated world, ethics still mattered most. Every AI-generated influencer partnership required transparent labeling. "Authenticity Mode" was activated automatically — ensuring any AI assistance or content modification was disclosed to audiences. Trust had become the most valuable commodity in the digital economy, and NovaBlend treated it like gold.

Midway through the year, NovaBlend tested a hybrid campaign blending real influencers with AI-generated virtual personalities. The virtual creators — built with photorealistic avatars and trained on brand voice — worked alongside human counterparts. The collaboration went viral, not because the avatars looked real, but because they were honest. The tagline read: *"AI created this, humans inspired it."*

During the annual summit, Elena presented NovaBlend's results to shareholders. "Our campaigns run 24/7, adapt automatically, and speak to every culture authentically," she said. “But what truly drives success is the collaboration between intelligence and empathy — between what AI understands and what humans feel.” The audience applauded, not for the technology, but for the philosophy.

That night, as the city lights reflected off her office window, Elena asked Atlas one final question: “What’s next for us?” The AI paused, then replied, “Deeper connection. Wider understanding. Greater creativity. Together.”

Elena smiled. She realized that influencer marketing had come full circle — from chaotic beginnings to algorithmic precision, and now to emotional partnership. AI hadn’t replaced creativity; it had expanded it. The future wasn’t machine-led or human-led — it was *collaboration-led.*

And as NovaBlend’s next campaign prepared to launch itself across six continents, Elena leaned back, confident that the fusion of intelligence and humanity had unlocked something extraordinary: influence that could evolve, adapt, and inspire — forever.

Epilogue

The Age of Intelligent Influence

Influencer marketing began as an experiment — an unpredictable art form powered by instinct, luck, and fleeting trends. It evolved through trial and error, guided by intuition and creativity but constrained by inefficiency. Then came artificial intelligence, quietly reshaping the foundation of how brands and creators connect, communicate, and collaborate. What once relied on manual outreach, emotional guesses, and slow analytics has become a disciplined science driven by automation, precision, and foresight. Yet, as this book has shown, the essence of influence has never been about technology alone — it has always been about trust, authenticity, and human connection. AI simply made those values scalable.

The journey through AI influencer marketing represents more than an evolution in marketing tools; it marks a fundamental shift in *how influence itself is understood.* For decades, influence was measured by numbers — followers, likes, clicks, and reach. AI redefined that understanding by uncovering the deeper layers beneath the metrics: emotion, sentiment, and intent. It taught brands to look beyond surface engagement and focus on resonance — on *why* people connect, *what* drives trust, and *how* authenticity translates into loyalty. The algorithms didn't replace relationships; they revealed what truly sustains them.

At every level of the modern marketing ecosystem, AI has brought clarity. It replaced guesswork with prediction, manual labor with automation, and isolated insights with holistic understanding. Through intelligent discovery systems, brands can now identify the right voices within seconds. Through AI-driven content analysis, they can understand what narratives inspire action. Through predictive ROI and smart budgeting, they can scale campaigns with confidence instead of hope. And through automated relationship management, they can nurture influencer partnerships that last years, not weeks. What was once a fragmented process is now a continuous, intelligent feedback loop — a living system that learns, adapts, and evolves with every interaction.

But even with all this progress, one truth remains unchanged: influence cannot exist without *authenticity*. The greatest challenge of the AI era is not technological — it's human. As machines take on the mechanics of marketing, creators and brands must double down on emotional honesty and ethical transparency. The audience of the future is not passive; it is perceptive, informed, and guided by values. They don't just want to be sold to — they want to believe, relate, and belong.

AI may predict their behaviors, but only genuine human connection can earn their trust. That is where the next generation of marketers will distinguish themselves — by combining intelligent systems with emotional intelligence.

The years ahead will introduce even more profound transformations. We will see **neural marketing models** capable of predicting engagement based on brainwave activity and emotional responses. **Voice AI systems** will co-create podcasts and narrations with influencers, blending tone and mood dynamically. **Virtual influencer ecosystems** will populate metaverse platforms, representing brands in immersive digital worlds. Yet, amid these technological marvels, the timeless principles will remain: authenticity, relevance, and empathy. The more advanced marketing becomes, the more it must remember the simple truth that people follow people — not algorithms.

For brands, this new landscape brings both opportunity and responsibility. The opportunity lies in reach — the ability to connect with millions in milliseconds. The responsibility lies in restraint — ensuring that automation serves humanity, not manipulates it. Ethical AI will become the foundation of sustainable influence. Every decision, from content generation to audience targeting, will require transparency, fairness, and respect for privacy. The brands that thrive in this future will not just use AI efficiently — they will use it *honorably*.

For influencers, the AI era offers empowerment. Instead of being at the mercy of unpredictable algorithms and ever-changing platforms, creators now have tools that analyze, optimize, and amplify their impact. AI provides insights that guide their artistic direction, automate their workflows, and monetize their creativity responsibly. It enables them to spend less time managing and more time creating. Yet the real gift AI offers creators is freedom — freedom to express their authenticity at scale, to connect across borders, and to build lasting influence based on purpose rather than pressure.

For marketers, the future role will be that of **architects of collaboration**. They will design ecosystems where AI handles the analytics, automation, and optimization — while humans provide intuition, empathy, and vision. The best campaigns will not be those that simply run efficiently, but those that blend logic with emotion, data with storytelling, and technology with humanity. AI will handle the precision; humans will provide the pulse. Together, they will define what it truly means to communicate with impact.

As we close this book, it's important to recognize that the AI revolution in influencer marketing is not an endpoint — it's the beginning of an entirely new discipline. The future will not belong to brands with the biggest budgets, but to those who can integrate intelligence and integrity seamlessly. It will belong to creators who use technology to deepen, not dilute, their connection with audiences. And it will belong to marketers who understand that every algorithm, no matter how advanced, still depends on one irreplaceable element: human purpose.

In this age of intelligent influence, we are witnessing the merging of art and science, emotion and computation, creativity and code. The marketers and influencers who embrace this balance — who lead with authenticity, guided by data and driven by purpose — will shape the next era of communication. AI may provide the blueprint, but humanity will always provide the meaning.

The future is already here — not cold, mechanical, or distant, but warm, human, and deeply connected. The tools of influence have changed forever, yet their ultimate goal remains the same: to inspire trust, evoke emotion, and create lasting impact. And now, with AI as both partner and guide, the power to do so has never been greater.

www.ingramcontent.com/pod-product-compliance
Lightning Source LLC
LaVergne TN
LVHW022010200926
848481LV00007B/2321
* 9 7 9 8 2 9 5 4 2 3 3 6 9 *